What in me is dark

Illumine

—JOHN MILTON

This book was given to

Dorothy & Carl

by

Hg & Lee

on

Your 50ᵗʰ Anniversary

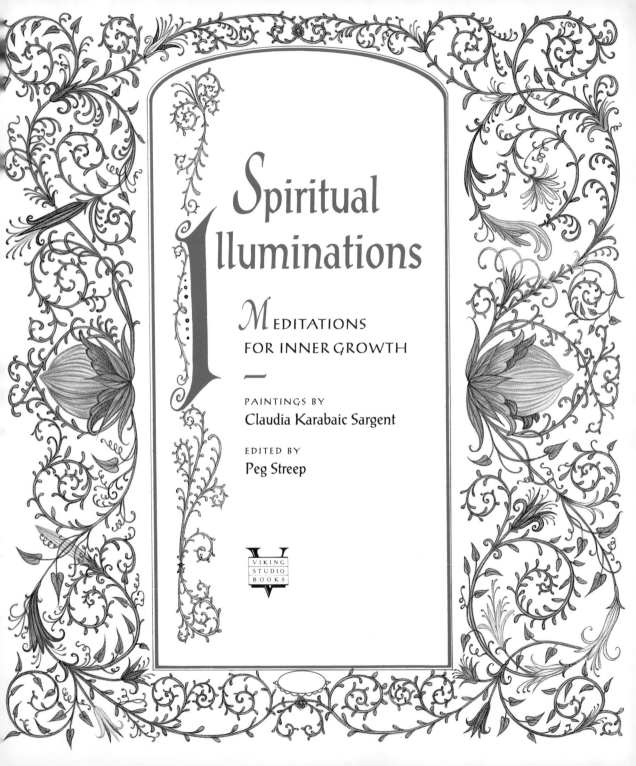

Spiritual Illuminations

Meditations for Inner Growth

PAINTINGS BY
Claudia Karabaic Sargent

EDITED BY
Peg Streep

VIKING
STUDIO
BOOKS

For the angels who watch over me, especially my grandmother, Angelina Papadimos; my grandfather, John
Karabaic; my teacher, Lorraine Fox D'Andrea; and my earth-angels, Frank and Felicity Rowfa.

—C.K.S.

For Alexandra, whose spirit informs mine every day, and for Peter, who is rightly named.

—P.S.

VIKING STUDIO BOOKS
Published by the Penguin Group
Viking Penguin, a division of Penguin Books USA Inc.,
375 Hudson Street, New York, New York 10014, U.S.A.
Penguin Books Ltd, 27 Wrights Lane, London W8 5TZ, England
Penguin Books Australia Ltd, Ringwood, Victoria, Australia
Penguin Books Canada Ltd, 10 Alcorn Avenue, Suite 300, Toronto, Ontario, Canada M4V 3B2
Penguin Books (N.Z.) Ltd, 182-190 Wairau Road, Auckland 10, New Zealand

Penguin Books Ltd., Registered Offices:
Harmondsworth, Middlesex, England

First published in 1992 by Viking Penguin, a division of Penguin Books USA Inc

3 5 7 9 10 8 6 4

LIBRARY OF CONGRESS CATALOGING IN PUBLICATION DATA
Spiritual illuminations: meditations for inner growth/
edited by Peg Streep: art by Claudia Karabaic Sargent
p. cm.
ISBN 0–670–84555–8
1. Meditations. 2. Spiritual life. I. Streep, Peg. II. Sargent, Claudia Karabaic.
BL624.2.I486 1992
291.4´3--dc20
92-54068

Printed in Japan
Set in Post Antiqua
Text design by Amy Hill and Kathryn Parise
Slipcase design by The Ladies

A PROMISED LAND PRODUCTION

INTRODUCTION

*A*rchaeology has shown us that humanity's recognition of the needs of the spirit is ancient indeed, although originally our spiritual gaze was directed at the earth—provider of life and of food—rather than at the sky. The spirit first found expression, thousands of years before the invention of written language, in images and carvings that served to articulate humanity's inner yearning and its relation to the larger whole, nature.

Millennia later, the inner spirit in all of us still beckons, by turns agitated and at rest, a source of strength and, sometimes, trouble. It is the musculature we sometimes forget to exercise, but in times of stress it is the armature, the resource, on which we all rely.

The journey of the spirit is rarely a linear one, a straight line between two points. The road along which the spirit travels is contradictory, even circular: sometimes a step forward entails a step back, sometimes learning requires unlearning, and remembering, forgetting.

Spiritual Illuminations has been created to nurture the spirit within, with art inspired by the centuries-old practice of illuminating manuscripts to accompany us as we travel the spiritual path. Its sections—"Gathering," "Meditation," "Renewal," and "Harmony"—echo the process of self-examination, thought, rebirth, and resolution that comprises spiritual renewal. We hope that the text selections, which reflect different voices, traditions, and centuries, will provide a starting point for *your* journey.

We have chosen the words of Ecclesiastes to unify this book, for we believe that they remind us of an important truth: that living is a process, that in every ending there is the promise of a new beginning, and that there *is* a time for every false step and a time for every right one.

—Peg Streep

CONTENTS

To every thing there is a season,
and a time to every purpose
under the heaven.

—ECCLESIASTES 3:1

Gathering

The leaves are falling, falling as from far,
as though above were withering farthest
gardens;
they fall with a denying attitude.

And night by night, down into solitude,
the heavy earth falls far from every star.

14

We are all falling. This hand's falling too—
all have this falling-sickness none
withstands.

And yet there's One whose gently-holding hands
this universal falling can't fall through.

—RAINER MARIA RILKE

15

Love is an act of faith,

and whoever is of little faith

is also of little love.

—Erich Fromm

The road to self-knowledge does not pass through faith. But only through the self-knowledge we gain by pursuing the fleeting light in the depth of our being do we reach the point where we can grasp what faith is. How many have been driven into outer darkness by empty talk about faith as something rationally comprehended, something "true."

—DAG HAMMARSKJÖLD

If I were looking for God, every event and every moment would sow, in my will, grains of His life, that would spring up one day in a tremendous harvest. For it is God's love that warms me in the sun and God's love that sends the cold rain. It is God's love that feeds me in the bread I eat and God that feeds me also by hunger and fasting. It is the love of God that sends the winter days when I am cold and sick, and the hot summer when I labor and my clothes are full of sweat: but it is God Who breathes on me with light winds off the river and in the breezes out of the wood. His love spreads the shade of the sycamore over my head and sends the water-boy along the edge of the

wheatfield with a bucket from the spring, while the laborers are resting and the mules stand under the tree.

It is God's love that speaks to me in the birds and streams but also behind the clamor of the city God speaks to me in His judgments, and all these things are seeds sent to me from His will.

If they would take root in my liberty, and if His will would grow from my freedom, I would become the love that He is, and my harvest would be His glory and my own joy.

And I would grow together with thousands and millions of other freedoms into the gold of one huge field praising God, loaded with increase, loaded with corn.

—THOMAS MERTON

Two roads diverged in a yellow wood,

And sorry I could not travel both

And be one traveler, long I stood

And looked down one as far as I could

To where it bent in the undergrowth;

Then took the other, as just as fair,

And having perhaps the better claim,

Because it was grassy and wanted wear;

Though as for that, the passing there

Had worn them really about the same,

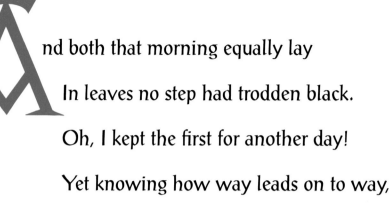

And both that morning equally lay

In leaves no step had trodden black.

Oh, I kept the first for another day!

Yet knowing how way leads on to way,

I doubted if I should ever come back.

I shall be telling this with a sigh

Somewhere ages and ages hence:

Two roads diverged in a wood, and I—

I took the one less traveled by,

And that has made all the difference.

—Robert Frost

I wake to sleep, and take my
    waking slow.
I feel my fate in what I cannot
    fear.
I learn by going where I have
    to go.

We think by feeling.
    What is there to know?
I hear my being dance from
    ear to ear.
I wake to sleep, and take my
    waking slow.

Of those so close beside me,
    which are you?
God bless the Ground!
    I shall walk softly there,
And learn by going where
    I have to go.

Light takes the Tree; but who can
    tell us how?
The lowly worm climbs up
    a winding stair;
I wake to sleep, and take my
    waking slow.

Great Nature has another thing
    to do
To you and me; so take the
    lively air,
And, lovely, learn by going
    where to go.

This shaking keeps me steady.
    I should know.
What falls away is always.
    And is near.
I wake to sleep, and take my
    waking slow.
I learn by going where I have
    to go.

—THEODORE ROETHKE

23

We have so little faith in the ebb and flow of life, of love, of relationships. We leap at the flow of the tide and resist in terror its ebb. We are afraid it will never return. We insist on permanency, on duration, on continuity; when the only continuity possible, in life as in love, is in growth, in fluidity—in freedom, in the sense that the dancers are free, barely touching as they pass, but partners in the same pattern. The only real security is not in owning or possessing, not in demanding or expecting, not in hoping, even. Security in a relationship lies neither in looking back to what it was in nostalgia, nor forward to what it might be in dread or anticipation, but living in the present relationship and accepting it as it is now. For relationships, too, must be like islands. One must accept them for what they are here and now, within their limits—islands, surrounded and interrupted by the sea, continually visited and abandoned by the tides. One must accept the security of the wingèd life, of ebb and flow, of intermittency.

Intermittency—an impossible lesson for human beings to learn. How can one learn to live through the ebb-tides of one's existence! How can one learn to take the trough of the wave! It is easier to understand here on the beach, where the breathlessly still ebb-tides reveal another life below the level which mortals usually reach. In this crystalline moment of suspense, one has a sudden revelation of the secret kingdom at the bottom of the sea. Here in the shallow flats one finds, wading through warm ripples, great horse-conchs pivoting on a leg; white sand dollars, marble medallions engraved in the mud; and myriads of bright-colored cochina-clams, glistening in the foam, their shells opening and shutting like butterflies' wings. So beautiful is the still hour of the sea's withdrawal, as beautiful as the sea's return when the encroaching waves pound up the beach, pressing to reach those dark rumpled chains of seaweed which mark the last high tide.

—ANNE MORROW LINDBERGH

This is thy hour O Soul,
thy free flight into the
wordless,
Away from books, away
from art, the day erased,
the lesson done,
Thee fully forth emerging,
silent, gazing, pondering
the themes thou lovest
best,
Night, sleep, death and
the stars.

—WALT WHITMAN

We and God have business with each other; and in opening ourselves to his influence our deepest destiny is fulfilled. The universe, at those parts of it which our personal being constitutes, takes a turn genuinely for the worse or for the better in proportion as each one of us fulfills or evades God's demands.

—WILLIAM JAMES

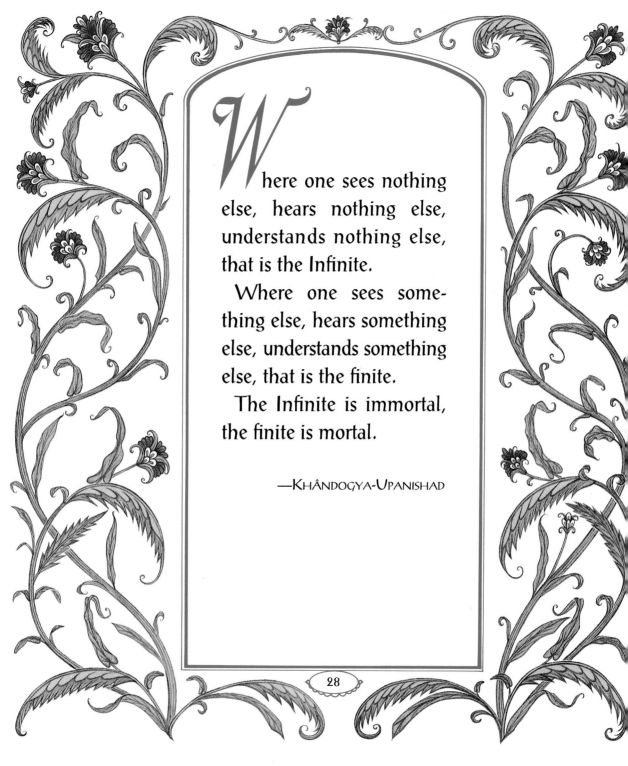

Where one sees nothing else, hears nothing else, understands nothing else, that is the Infinite.

Where one sees something else, hears something else, understands something else, that is the finite.

The Infinite is immortal, the finite is mortal.

—Khândogya-Upanishad

28

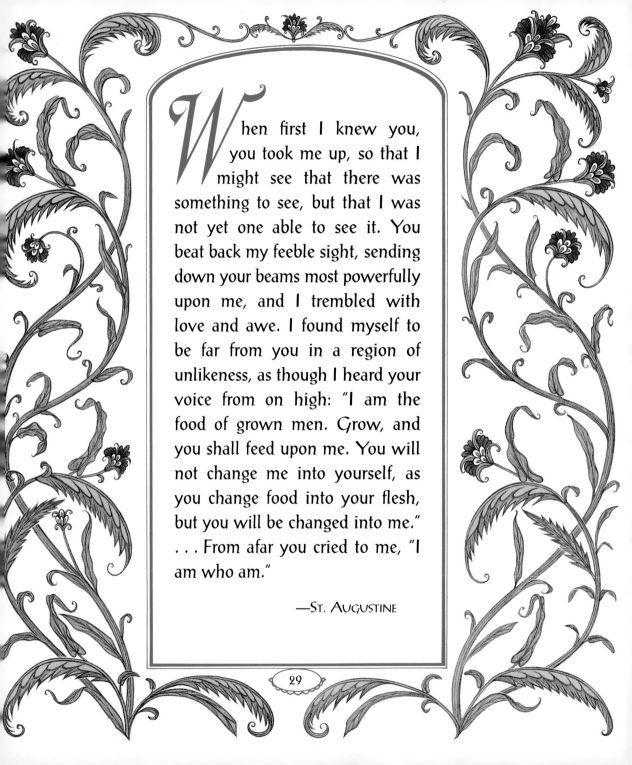

When first I knew you, you took me up, so that I might see that there was something to see, but that I was not yet one able to see it. You beat back my feeble sight, sending down your beams most powerfully upon me, and I trembled with love and awe. I found myself to be far from you in a region of unlikeness, as though I heard your voice from on high: "I am the food of grown men. Grow, and you shall feed upon me. You will not change me into yourself, as you change food into your flesh, but you will be changed into me." . . . From afar you cried to me, "I am who am."

—St. Augustine

29

All perfection in this life is accompanied by a measure of imperfection, and all our knowledge contains an element of obscurity.

—Thomas à Kempis

God offers to every mind its choice between truth and repose. Take which you please,—you can never have both. Between these, as a pendulum, man oscillates. He in whom the love of repose predominates will accept the first creed, the first philosophy, the first political party he meets,—most likely his father's. He gets rest, commodity, and reputation; but he shuts the door of truth. He in whom the love of truth predominates will keep himself aloof from all the moorings, and afloat. He will abstain from dogmatism, and recognize all the opposite negations between which, as walls, his being is swung. He submits to the inconvenience of suspense and imperfect opinion, but he is a candidate for truth, as the other is not, and respects the highest law of his being.

—Ralph Waldo Emerson

dust as we are, the immortal spirit grows
   Like harmony in music; there is a dark
   Inscrutable workmanship that reconciles
   Discordant elements, makes them cling together
   In one society. How strange that all
   The terrors, pains, and early miseries,
   Regrets, vexations, lassitudes interfused
   Within my mind, should e'er have borne a part,
   And that a needful part, in making up
   The calm existence that is mine when I
   Am worthy of myself!

—WILLIAM WORDSWORTH

The best knowledge that we have of God here, even by faith, is rather that he knows us, than that we know him.

—John Donne

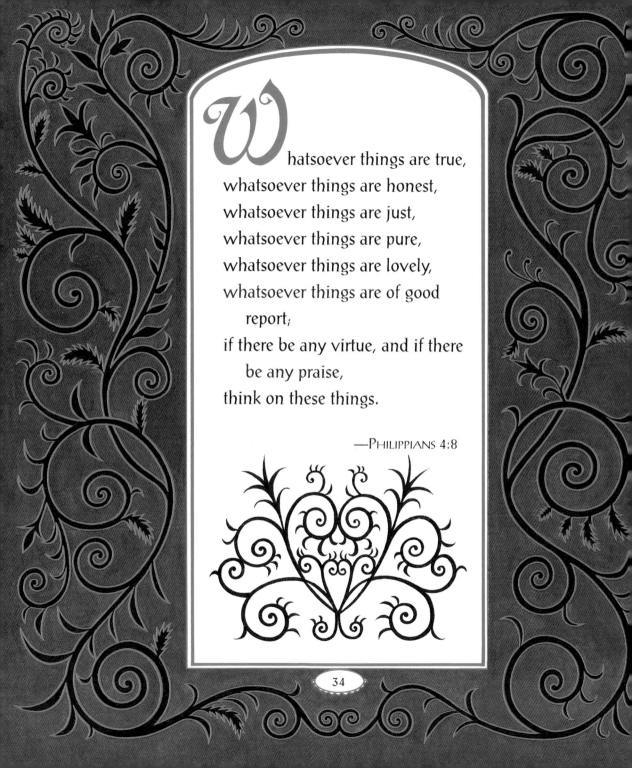

Whatsoever things are true,
whatsoever things are honest,
whatsoever things are just,
whatsoever things are pure,
whatsoever things are lovely,
whatsoever things are of good
    report;
if there be any virtue, and if there
    be any praise,
think on these things.

—Philippians 4:8

34

The kingdom of God cometh
not with observation;
Neither shall they say, Lo here! or,
Lo there! for behold, the kingdom
of God is within you.

—LUKE 17:20–21

A time to be born, and a time to die;
    a time to plant, and a time to pluck up that which is planted;
A time to kill, and a time to heal; a time to break down,
    and a time to build up;
A time to weep, and a time to laugh; a time to mourn,
    and a time to dance.

—ECCLESIASTES 3:2–4

Meditation

god be in my head,
And in my understanding;

god be in my eyes,
And in my looking;

god be in my mouth,
And in my speaking;

god be in my heart,
And in my thinking;

god be at my end,
And at my departing.

—*SARUM
MISSAL*

God, grant me the serenity to
accept the things I cannot
change;
the courage to change the
things I can;
and the wisdom to know the
difference.

—"The Serenity Prayer"

39

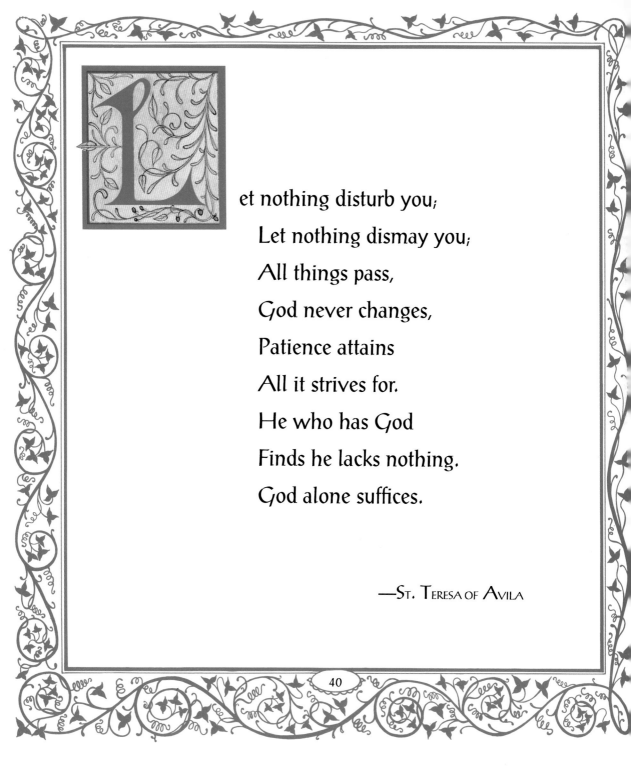

Let nothing disturb you;
Let nothing dismay you;
All things pass,
God never changes,
Patience attains
All it strives for.
He who has God
Finds he lacks nothing.
God alone suffices.

—St. Teresa of Avila

et pain is part of being alive, and we need to learn that. Pain does not last forever, nor is it necessarily unbearable, and we need to be taught that. Adolescents need to accept the fact that broken hearts, like broken bones, hurt dreadfully but ultimately they heal, and that there is life beyond the hurting. People whose shameful secret is about to be revealed need to be assured that there is forgiveness as well as condemnation, that there are people in the world and a God in the world capable of forgiving and loving even the most flawed and imperfect of us. The terminally ill need to be reassured that we will cherish them and spend time with them and take them as seriously as we did when they were healthy. Most of all, we have to learn to trust our own capacities to endure pain. We can endure much more than we think we can; all human experience testifies to that. All we need to do is learn not to be afraid of pain. Grit your teeth and let it hurt. Don't deny it, don't be overwhelmed by it. It will not last forever. One day, the pain will be gone and you will still be there.

—HAROLD S. KUSHNER

Our ordinary waking life is a bare existence in which, most of the time, we seem to be absent from ourselves and from reality because we are involved in the vain preoccupations which dog the steps of every living man. But there are times when we seem suddenly to awake and discover the full meaning of our own present reality. Such discoveries are not capable of being contained in formulas or definitions. They are a matter of personal experience, of incommunicable intuition. In the light of such an experience it is easy to see the futility of all the trifles that occupy our minds. We recapture something of the calm and the balance that ought always to be ours, and we understand that life is far too great a gift to be squandered on anything less than perfection.

In the lives of those who are adrift in the modern world, with nothing to rely on but their own resources, these moments of understanding

are short-lived and barren. For, though man may get a glimpse of the natural value of his spirit, nature alone is incapable of fulfilling his spiritual aspirations.

   The Truth man needs is not a philosopher's abstraction but God Himself. The paradox of contemplation is that God is never really known unless He is also loved. And we cannot love Him unless we do His will. This explains why modern man, who knows so much, is nevertheless ignorant. Because he is without love, modern man fails to see the only Truth that matters and on which all else depends.

—THOMAS MERTON

There is a solitude of space
    A solitude of sea
    A solitude of death,
        but these
    Society shall be
    Compared with that
        profounder site
    That polar privacy
    A soul admitted to itself—
    Finite infinity.

—EMILY DICKINSON

A noiseless patient spider,
   I mark'd where on a little promontory it stood isolated,
   Mark'd how to explore the vacant vast surrounding,
   It launch'd forth filament, filament, filament, out of itself,
   Ever unreeling them, ever tirelessly speeding them.

And you O my soul where you stand,
   Surrounded, detached, in measureless oceans of space,
   Ceaselessly musing, venturing, throwing, seeking the
      spheres to connect them,
   Till the bridge you will need be form'd, till the ductile
      anchor hold,
   Till the gossamer thread you fling catch somewhere,
      O my soul.

—WALT WHITMAN

45

Coming out of darkness
   I'm likely to enter
   The darker path again.
   Shine far all over,
   Moon on the mountain edge.

In the dark
   I lost sight of
   My shadow;
   I've found it again
   By the fire I lit.

When I see
   Heaven and earth as
   My own garden,
   I live that moment
   Outside the universe.

Wind is your breath;
    The open sky, your mind
    The sun, your eye;
    Seas and mountains,
    Your whole body.

The One Mind
    Of heaven and earth
    Is dyed into
    A thousand different
    Grass colors.

—A Zen Harvest

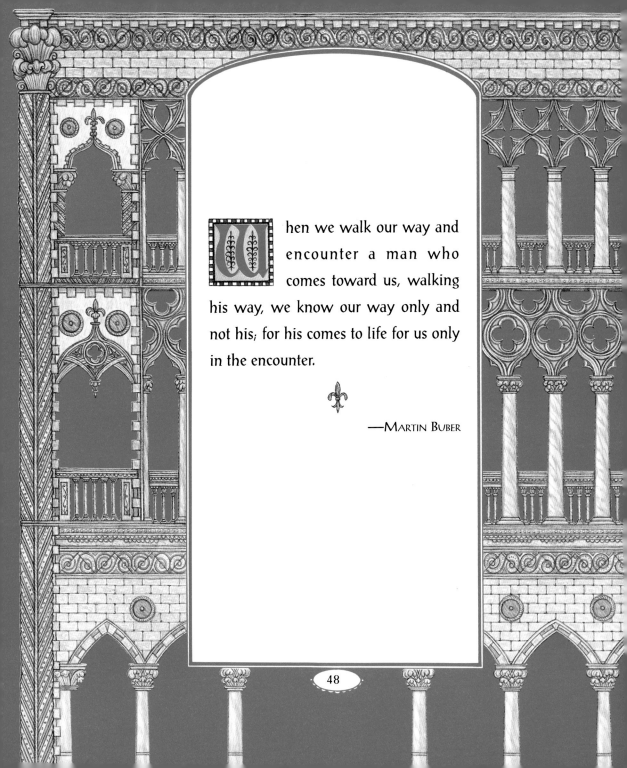

When we walk our way and encounter a man who comes toward us, walking his way, we know our way only and not his; for his comes to life for us only in the encounter.

—MARTIN BUBER

48

For it is not physical solitude that actually separates one from other men, not physical isolation, but spiritual isolation. It is not the desert island nor the stony wilderness that cuts you from the people you love. It is the wilderness in the mind, the desert wastes in the heart through which one wanders lost and a stranger. When one is a stranger to oneself then one is estranged from others too. If one is out of touch with oneself, then one cannot touch others.

—ANNE MORROW LINDBERGH

an is but a reed, the weakest thing in nature; but a thinking reed. It does not need the universe to take up arms to crush him; a vapour, a drop of water, is enough to kill him. But, though the universe should crush him, man would still be nobler than his destroyer, because he knows that he is dying, knows that the universe has got the better of him; the universe knows naught of that.

All our dignity then consists in thought. We must look to that in order to rise aloft; not to space or time which we can never fill. Strive we then to think aright: that is the first principle of moral life.

—BLAISE PASCAL

never look down to test the ground before taking your next step: only he who keeps his eye fixed on the far horizon will find his right road.

never measure the height of a mountain, until you have reached the top. Then you will see how low it was.

—Dag Hammarskjöld

Incline your ear,

and come unto me;

hear, and your soul

shall live.

—Isaiah 55:3

The universe, open to the eye to-day, looks as it did a thousand years ago. . . . We see what all our fathers saw. And if we cannot find God in your house or in mine, upon the roadside or the margin of the sea; in the bursting seed or opening flower; in the day duty or the night musing; in the general laugh and the secret grief; in the procession of life, ever entering afresh, and solemnly passing by and dropping off; I do not think we should discern him any more on the grass of Eden, or beneath the moonlight of Gethsemane.

—JAMES MARTINEAU

53

To have faith requires *courage*, the ability to take a risk, the readiness even to accept pain and disappointment. Whoever insists on safety and security as primary conditions of life cannot have faith; whoever shuts himself off in a system of defense, where distance and possession are his means of security, makes himself a prisoner. To be loved, and to love, need courage, the courage to judge certain values as of ultimate concern—and to take the jump and stake everything on these values.

—ERICH FROMM

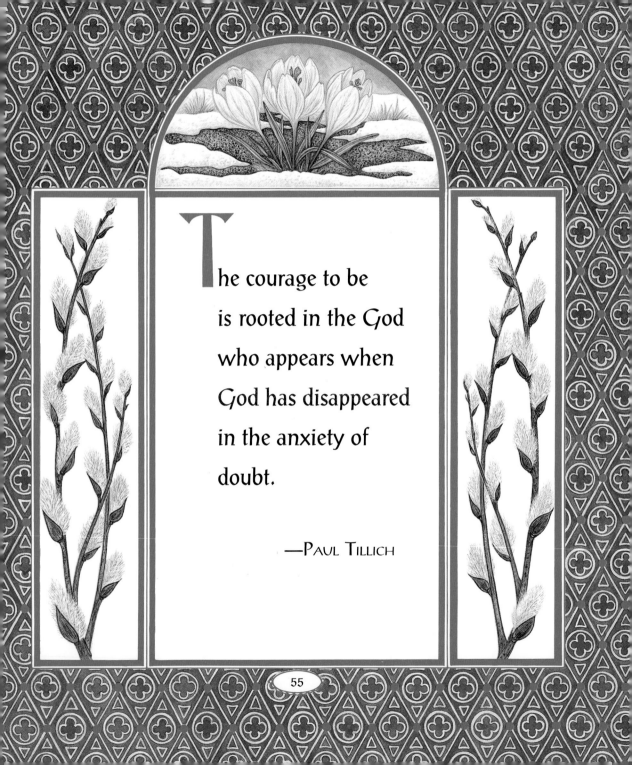

The courage to be
is rooted in the God
who appears when
God has disappeared
in the anxiety of
doubt.

—PAUL TILLICH

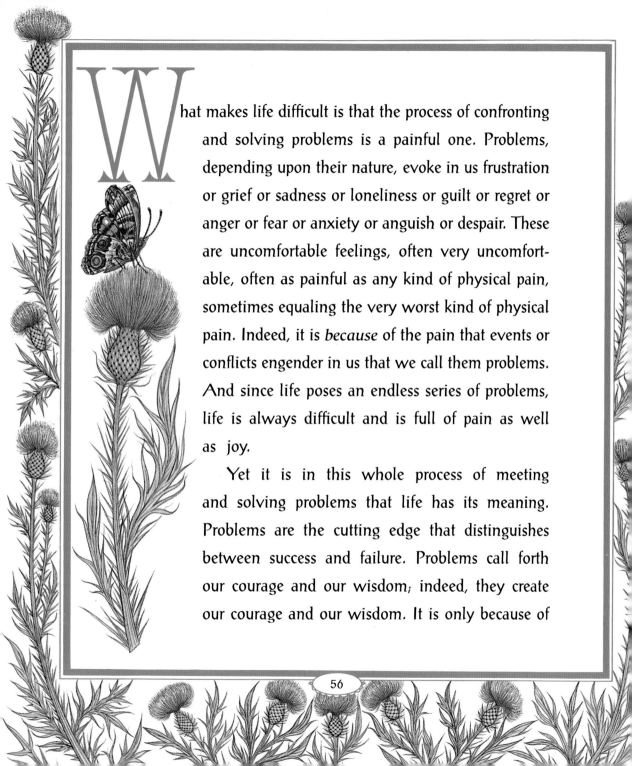

What makes life difficult is that the process of confronting and solving problems is a painful one. Problems, depending upon their nature, evoke in us frustration or grief or sadness or loneliness or guilt or regret or anger or fear or anxiety or anguish or despair. These are uncomfortable feelings, often very uncomfortable, often as painful as any kind of physical pain, sometimes equaling the very worst kind of physical pain. Indeed, it is *because* of the pain that events or conflicts engender in us that we call them problems. And since life poses an endless series of problems, life is always difficult and is full of pain as well as joy.

Yet it is in this whole process of meeting and solving problems that life has its meaning. Problems are the cutting edge that distinguishes between success and failure. Problems call forth our courage and our wisdom; indeed, they create our courage and our wisdom. It is only because of

problems that we grow mentally and spiritually. When we desire to encourage the growth of the human spirit, we challenge and encourage the human capacity to solve problems, just as in school we deliberately set problems for our children to solve. It is through the pain of confronting and resolving problems that we learn. As Benjamin Franklin said, "Those things that hurt, instruct." It is for this reason that wise people learn not to dread but actually to welcome problems and actually to welcome the pain of problems.

—M. SCOTT PECK, M.D.

Not only in our personal lives, but also in the life of humanity we must have the ability to live in long-term values instead of short-time values. We should know that the defeat of the moment is not the defeat of eternity, that civilization is a tougher plant than we usually imagine. It has its roots widely scattered over the surface of the earth, and even when the drought of war comes as a blight to wither some of its tendrils, nevertheless it sends forth bud and blossom and rich fruit in other climates and in other times. We who live through an age of fire and hail and snow are often too much overwhelmed to feel the coming of new life beneath our feet and the promise of a new

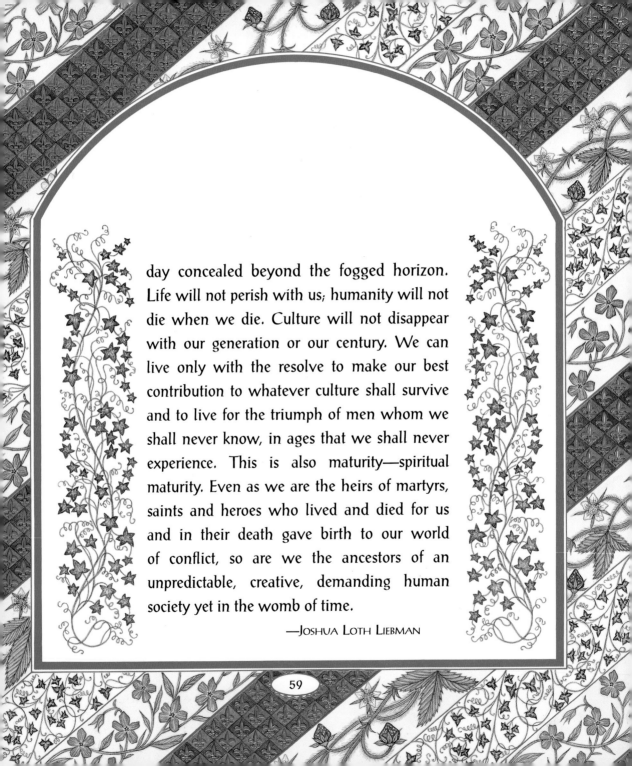

day concealed beyond the fogged horizon. Life will not perish with us; humanity will not die when we die. Culture will not disappear with our generation or our century. We can live only with the resolve to make our best contribution to whatever culture shall survive and to live for the triumph of men whom we shall never know, in ages that we shall never experience. This is also maturity—spiritual maturity. Even as we are the heirs of martyrs, saints and heroes who lived and died for us and in their death gave birth to our world of conflict, so are we the ancestors of an unpredictable, creative, demanding human society yet in the womb of time.

—JOSHUA LOTH LIEBMAN

god's silence ripens man's thoughts into speech.

Every child comes with the message that God is not yet discouraged of man.

The leaf becomes flower when it loves.
The flower becomes fruit when it worships.

The dust of the dead words
clings to thee.
Wash thy soul with silence.

—RABINDRANATH
TAGORE

A time to cast away stones, and a time to gather stones together; a time to embrace, and a time to refrain from embracing; A time to get, and a time to lose; a time to keep, and a time to cast away.

—ECCLESIASTES 3:5–6

Renewal

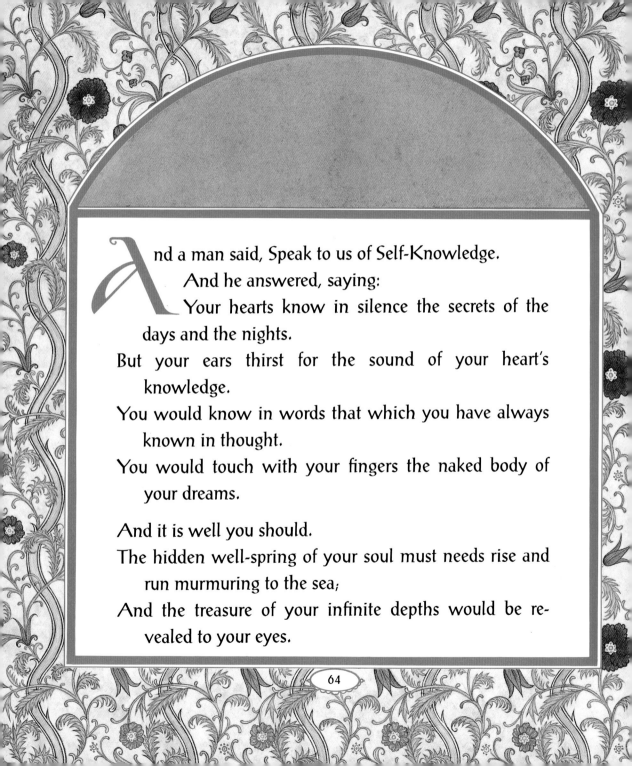

And a man said, Speak to us of Self-Knowledge.

And he answered, saying:

Your hearts know in silence the secrets of the days and the nights.

But your ears thirst for the sound of your heart's knowledge.

You would know in words that which you have always known in thought.

You would touch with your fingers the naked body of your dreams.

And it is well you should.

The hidden well-spring of your soul must needs rise and run murmuring to the sea;

And the treasure of your infinite depths would be revealed to your eyes.

But let there be no scales to weigh your unknown treasure;
And seek not the depths of your knowledge with staff or
    sounding line.
For self is a sea boundless and measureless.

Say not, "I have found the truth," but rather, "I have
    found a truth."
Say not, "I have found the path of the soul." Say rather, "I
    have met the soul walking upon my path."
For the soul walks upon all paths.
The soul walks not upon a line, neither does it grow like
    a reed.
The soul unfolds itself, like a lotus of countless petals.

—KAHLIL GIBRAN

shall sing praises now that the time of the singing of birds has come, and I shall answer in song: go in peace, rain. I shall look at the deeds of my God, so pleasant in their season, and sweetly say: come in peace, dew. The rains are over and gone, the winter is past; everything is created with beauty: go in peace, rain. The mandrakes give forth their perfume in the lovers' garden; sorrows are past: come in peace, dew. The earth is crowned with new grain and wine, and every creature cries: go in peace, rain!

—ANONYMOUS

erciful God—

    This is a wondrous thing; that if she touch

    My fingernail with but her fingernail,—

    Or if she look at me, for but the time

    It takes a leaf to fall from leaf to leaf,—

    I become music, chaos, light, and sound;

    I am no longer I: I am a world.

—Conrad Aiken

A child said *What is the grass?*
fetching it to me with full
hands;
How could I answer the child? I
do not know what it is any more
than he.

I guess it must be the flag of my
disposition, out of hopeful green
stuff woven.

Or I guess it is the handkerchief of the
Lord,
A scented gift and remembrancer
designedly dropt,
Bearing the owner's name someway
in the corners, that we may see and
remark, and say *Whose?*

—WALT WHITMAN

To study hard, think quietly, talk gently, act frankly; to listen to stars and birds, to babes and sages, with open heart; to bear all cheerfully, do all bravely, await occasions, hurry never. In a word to let the spiritual, unbidden and unconscious, grow up through the common. This to be my symphony.

—WILLIAM HENRY CHANNING

69

I remember one day in early spring, I was alone in the forest, lending my ear to its mysterious noises. I listened, and my thought went back to what for these three years it always was busy with—the quest of God. But the idea of him, I said, how did I ever come by the idea?

And again there arose in me, with this thought, glad aspirations towards life. Everything in me awoke and received a meaning . . . Why do I look farther? a voice within me asked. He is there: he, without whom one cannot live. To acknowledge God and to live are one and the same thing. God is what life is.

—LEO TOLSTOY

For God hath not given us the spirit of fear;
but of power, and of love, and of
a sound mind.

—II TIMOTHY 1:7

lory be to God for dappled things—
  For skies of couple-colour as a brinded
    cow;
  For rose-moles all in stipple upon trout
    that swim;

resh-firecoal chestnut-falls; finches' wings;
  Landscape plotted and pieced—fold, fallow,
    and plough;
  And àll tràdes, their gear and tackle and
    trim.

all things counter, original, spare, strange;
  Whatever is fickle, freckled (who knows
    how?)
  With swift, slow; sweet, sour; adazzle,
    dim;

be fathers-forth whose beauty is past change:
  Praise him.

—GERARD MANLEY HOPKINS

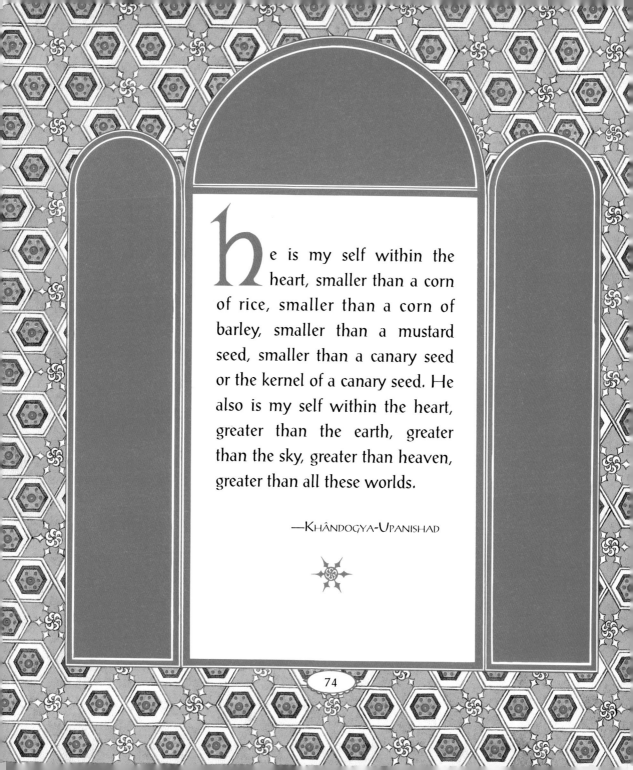

he is my self within the heart, smaller than a corn of rice, smaller than a corn of barley, smaller than a mustard seed, smaller than a canary seed or the kernel of a canary seed. He also is my self within the heart, greater than the earth, greater than the sky, greater than heaven, greater than all these worlds.

—Khândogya-Upanishad

74

O Our Mother the Earth, O Our
Father the Sky
Your children are we and with
tired backs
We bring you the gifts you love.
Then weave for us a garment of
brightness
May the warp be the white light of
morning
May the weft be the red light of
evening
May the fringes be the falling rain
May the border be the standing
rainbow.
Thus weave for us a garment of
brightness
That we may walk fittingly where
grass is green
O Our Mother the Earth, O Our
Father the Sky.

—Tewe Song

These roses under my window make no reference to former roses or to better ones; they are for what they are; they exist with God today. There is no time to them. There is simply the rose; it is perfect in every moment of its existence. Before a leaf-bud has burst, its whole life acts; in the full-blown flower there is no more; in the leafless root there is no less. Its nature is satisfied and it satisfies nature in all moments alike.

—Ralph Waldo Emerson

To recognize that failure at times is the common lot of all men, to see in ourselves and in others the traces of the primitive as well as the promise of the civilized, to admit that our friends' patterns of life, although different from ours, are equally valuable, and because of the very differences indispensable for a rich and varied universe, to recognize that another may be right while we are wrong, is to attain the second great need of individual adjustment—genuine inner tolerance.

—Joshua Loth Liebman

To yield is to be preserved whole.

To be bent is to become straight.

To be empty is to be full.

To be worn out is to be renewed.

To have little is to possess.

—LAO-TZU

78

There are two ways of spreading light:

to be the candle or the mirror

that reflects it.

—EDITH WHARTON

i am a little church (no great cathedral)
  far from the splendor and squalor of hurrying cities
  —i do not worry if briefer days grow briefest,
  i am not sorry when sun and rain make april

  my life is the life of the reaper and the sower;
  my prayers are prayers of earth's own clumsily striving
  (finding and losing and laughing and crying) children
  whose any sadness or joy is my grief or my gladness

  around me surges a miracle of unceasing
  birth and glory and death and resurrection:
  over my sleeping self float flaming symbols
  of hope, and i wake to a perfect patience of mountains

i am a little church (far from the frantic
world with its rapture and anguish) at peace with nature
—i do not worry if longer nights grow longest;
i am not sorry when silence becomes singing

winter by spring, i lift my diminutive spire to
merciful Him Whose only now is forever:
standing erect in the deathless truth of His presence
(welcoming humbly His light and proudly His darkness)

—E. E. CUMMINGS

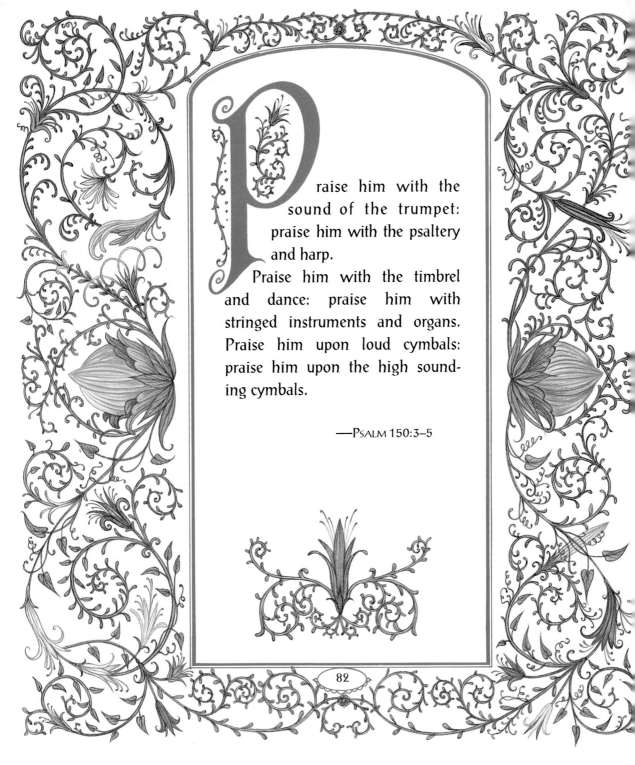

Praise him with the sound of the trumpet: praise him with the psaltery and harp.

Praise him with the timbrel and dance: praise him with stringed instruments and organs. Praise him upon loud cymbals: praise him upon the high sounding cymbals.

—Psalm 150:3–5

Yet a little while is the light with you. Walk while ye have the light, lest darkness come upon you; for he that walketh in darkness knoweth not whither he goeth. While ye have light, believe in the light, that ye may be the children of light.

—JOHN 12:35–36

83

84

Alleluia!

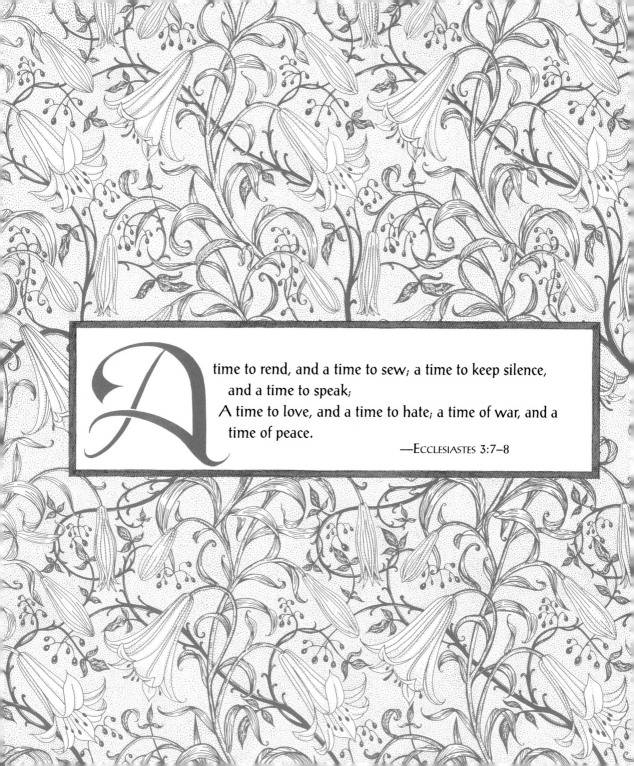

A time to rend, and a time to sew; a time to keep silence, and a time to speak;
A time to love, and a time to hate; a time of war, and a time of peace.

—ECCLESIASTES 3:7–8

Harmony

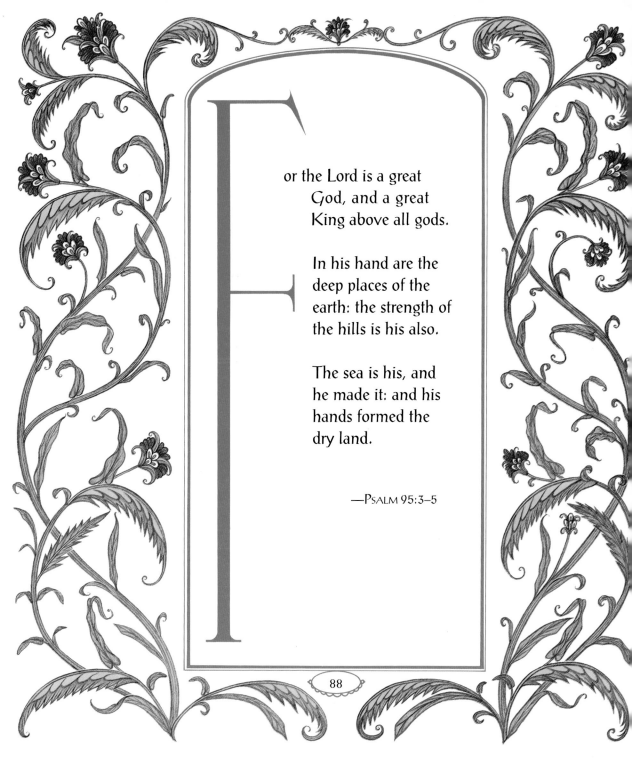

For the Lord is a great
God, and a great
King above all gods.

In his hand are the
deep places of the
earth: the strength of
the hills is his also.

The sea is his, and
he made it: and his
hands formed the
dry land.

—PSALM 95:3–5

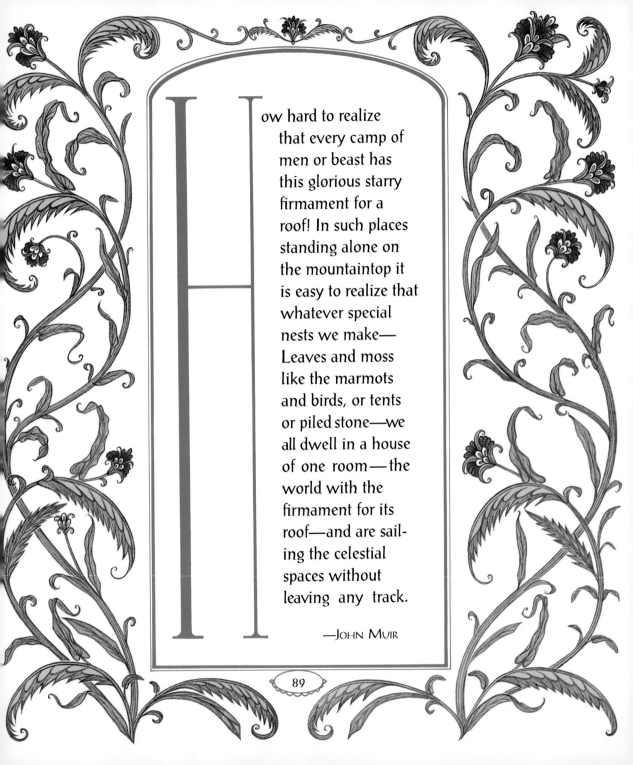

How hard to realize that every camp of men or beast has this glorious starry firmament for a roof! In such places standing alone on the mountaintop it is easy to realize that whatever special nests we make— Leaves and moss like the marmots and birds, or tents or piled stone—we all dwell in a house of one room—the world with the firmament for its roof—and are sailing the celestial spaces without leaving any track.

—JOHN MUIR

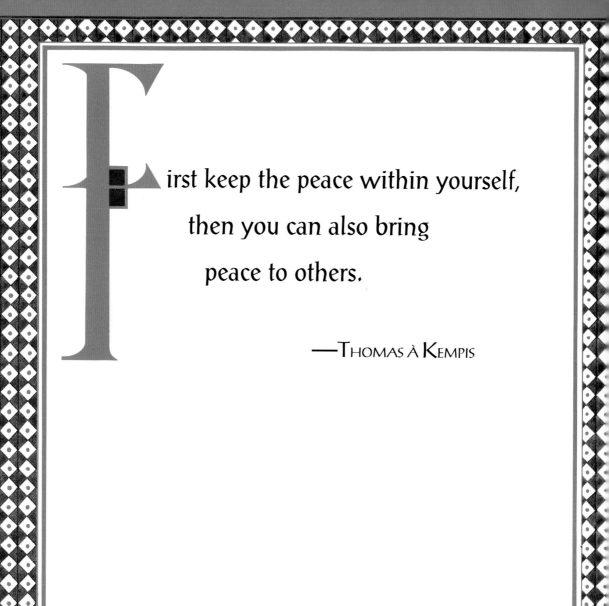

First keep the peace within yourself,

then you can also bring

peace to others.

—Thomas à Kempis

Lord, make me an instrument of Your peace.
Where there is hatred, let me sow love;
where there is injury, pardon;
where there is doubt, faith;
where there is despair, hope;
where there is darkness, light;
and where there is sadness, joy.

O divine Master, grant that I may not so much
seek to be consoled as to console;
to be understood as to understand;
to be loved as to love.
For it is in giving that we receive;
it is in pardoning that we are pardoned;
and it is in dying that we are born
to eternal life.

—St. Francis of Assisi

There is no need to run outside
  For better seeing,
Nor to peer from a window.
  Rather abide
At the center of your being;
For the more you leave it, the less
  you learn.
Search your heart and see
If he is wise who takes each turn:
The way to do is to be.

—Lao-tzu

Swiftly arose and spread around
me the peace and knowledge
that pass all the argument of
the earth,
And I know that the hand of God
is the promise of my own,
And I know that the spirit of God
is the brother of my own,
And that all the men ever born are
also my brothers, and the women
my sisters and lovers,
And that a kelson of the creation
is love,
And limitless are leaves stiff or
drooping in the field...

—WALT WHITMAN

93

There is no object that we see,

no action that we do,

no good that we enjoy,

no evil that we feel or fear,

but that we may make some

spiritual advantage of all.

—ANNE BRADSTREET

Do all the good you can,

By all the means you can,

In all the ways you can,

In all the places you can,

At all the times you can,

To all the people you can,

As long as ever you can.

—JOHN WESLEY

...I always think that the best way to know God is to love many things. Love a friend, a wife, something—whatever you like— you will be on the way to knowing more about Him; that is what I say to myself. But one must love with a lofty and serious intimate sympathy, with strength, with intelligence; and one must always try to know deeper, better and more. That leads to God, that leads to un- wavering faith.

—VINCENT VAN GOGH

I had long known the diverse
  tastes of the wood,
Each leaf, each bark, rank earth
  from every hollow;
Knew the smells of bird's
  breath and of bat's wing;
Yet sight I lacked: until you
  stole upon me,
Touching my eyelids with light
  finger-tips.
The trees blazed out, their
  colours whirled together,
Nor ever before had I been
  aware of sky.

—Robert Graves

97

or once we perceive the reality of grace, our understanding of ourselves as meaningless and insignificant is shattered. The fact that there exists beyond ourselves and our conscious will a powerful force that nurtures our growth and evolution is enough to turn our notions of self-insignificance topsy-turvy. For the existence of this force (once we perceive it) indicates with incontrovertible certainty that our human spiritual growth is of the utmost importance to something greater than ourselves. This something we call God. The existence of grace is *prima facie* evidence not only of the reality of God but also of the reality that God's will is devoted to the growth of the individual human spirit. What once seemed to be a fairy tale turns out to be the reality.

We live our lives in the eye of God, and not at the periphery but at the center of His vision, His concern. It is probable that the universe as we know it is but a single stepping-stone toward the entrance to the Kingdom of God. But we are hardly lost in the universe. To the contrary, the reality of grace indicates humanity to be at the center of the universe.

—M. Scott Peck, M.D.

That you need God more than anything, you know at all times in your heart. But don't you know also that God needs you—in the fullness of his eternity, you? How would man exist if God did not need him, and how would you exist? You need God in order to be, and God needs you—for that which is the meaning of your life.

—MARTIN BUBER

do not say, "It is morning," and dismiss it with a name of yesterday. See it for the first time as a new-born child that has no name.

—RABINDRANATH TAGORE

i thank You God for most this amazing
        day: for the leaping greenly spirits of trees
        and a blue true dream of sky; and for everything
        which is natural which is infinite which is yes

        (i who have died am alive again today,
        and this is the sun's birthday; this is the birth
        day of life and of love and wings: and of the gay
        great happening illimitably earth)

        how should tasting touching hearing seeing
        breathing any—lifted from the no
        of all nothing—human merely being
        doubt unimaginable You?

        (now the ears of my ears awake and
        now the eyes of my eyes are opened)

—E. E. CUMMINGS

Our Father which art in
heaven,
Hallowed be thy name.
Thy kingdom come.
Thy will be done
in earth, as it is in
heaven.
Give us this day our
daily bread.
And forgive us our
debts,
as we forgive our
debtors.

And lead us not into
temptation, but deliver
us from evil:
For thine is the kingdom,
and the power, and the
glory, for ever.   Amen.

—MATTHEW 6:9–13

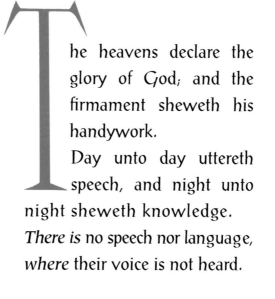

The heavens declare the glory of God; and the firmament sheweth his handywork.

Day unto day uttereth speech, and night unto night sheweth knowledge.

There is no speech nor language, *where* their voice is not heard.

—Psalm 19:1–2

For now we see through a glass, darkly; but then face to face; now I know in part; but then shall I know even as also I am known.

And now abideth faith, hope, charity, these three; but the greatest of these is charity.

—I CORINTHIANS 13:12–13

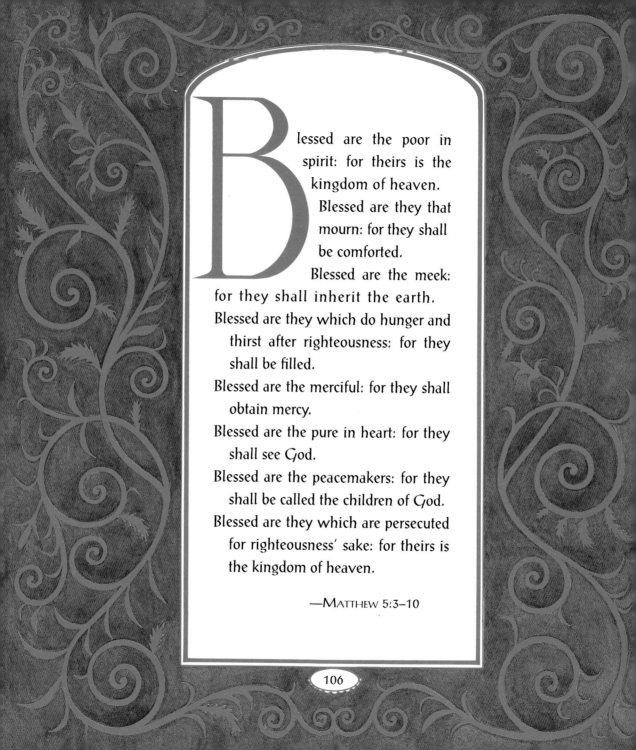

Blessed are the poor in spirit: for theirs is the kingdom of heaven.

Blessed are they that mourn: for they shall be comforted.

Blessed are the meek: for they shall inherit the earth.

Blessed are they which do hunger and thirst after righteousness: for they shall be filled.

Blessed are the merciful: for they shall obtain mercy.

Blessed are the pure in heart: for they shall see God.

Blessed are the peacemakers: for they shall be called the children of God.

Blessed are they which are persecuted for righteousness' sake: for theirs is the kingdom of heaven.

—MATTHEW 5:3–10

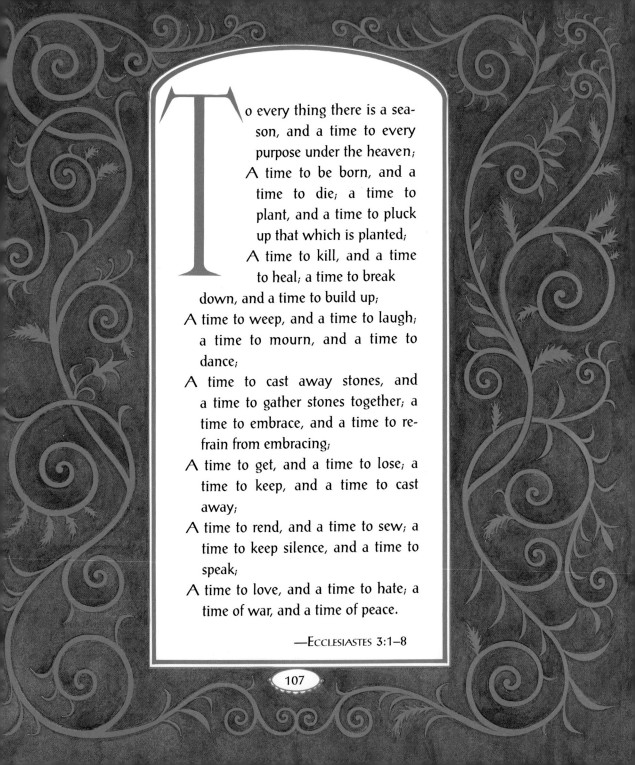

To every thing there is a season, and a time to every purpose under the heaven;
A time to be born, and a time to die; a time to plant, and a time to pluck up that which is planted;
A time to kill, and a time to heal; a time to break down, and a time to build up;
A time to weep, and a time to laugh; a time to mourn, and a time to dance;
A time to cast away stones, and a time to gather stones together; a time to embrace, and a time to refrain from embracing;
A time to get, and a time to lose; a time to keep, and a time to cast away;
A time to rend, and a time to sew; a time to keep silence, and a time to speak;
A time to love, and a time to hate; a time of war, and a time of peace.

—Ecclesiastes 3:1–8